5-Ingredient Recipes

Super Quick and Simple Budget-Friendly Recipes for Delicious Meals

Leslie Joy

work can be in any fashion deemed liable for any hardship or damages that may befall them after undertaking information described herein.

Additionally, the information in the following pages is intended only for informational purposes and should thus be thought of as universal. As befitting its nature, it is presented without assurance regarding its prolonged validity or interim quality. Trademarks that are mentioned are done without written consent and can in no way be considered an endorsement from the trademark holder.

TABLE OF CONTENTS

INTRODUCTION.. 7

5-INGREDIENT RECIPES 9

    Cauliflower Toast with Avocado 10

    Almond Butter Brownies.. 12

    Pumpkin Pancakes... 13

    Kale Smoothie... 14

    Tiramisu Chia Pudding.. 15

    Apple - Lemon Bowl... 16

    Bacon Mini Frittata 17

    Chocolate Peanut Butter Shake 18

    Ham Muffins... 19

    Nori Salmon Handroll 20

    Breakfast Cheesy Sausage 21

    Crusty Grilled Corn.. 22

    Creamy Potato Spread.. 23

    Garlic and Kale Platter.. 24

    Almond Bread... 25

    Mozzarella Chips 26

    Broccoli Stir Fry.. 27

    Wrapped Plums 28

    Fried Apple 29

    Paprika Sweet Potato 30

    Tomato Basil Spaghetti 31

Worcestershire Pork Chops...32

Baked Chicken Wings...33

Broccoli Bacon Salad with Onions and Coconut Cream 34

Thyme and Lemon Couscous..35

Sage Salmon Fillet 36

Eggs Baked in an Avocado 37

Shrimp Ginger Cucumber with Fried Rice...............................38

5 Ingredients Pasta..39

French Onion Soup...41

Cream of Mushroom Soup...42

Grilled Eggplant Steaks..43

Coconut Chicken 44

Shrimp and Broccoli..46

Tofu Nuggets with Barbecue Glaze......................................47

Yummy Turkey Meatballs 48

Healthy Poached Trout 50

Avocado Cucumber Soup 51

Oregano and Pesto Lamb 52

Buttery Shrimp...53

Salted Caramel Chocolate Cups 54

Warm Peach Compote...55

Vanilla Custard 56

Peanut Brittle 57

Watermelon Mint Popsicles..58

Creamy Strawberries *59*

Coconut Bars *60*

Boston Baked Beans Candy *61*

Chocolate Rice *62*

Greek Yogurt Muesli Parfaits *63*

Introduction

Make healthy and easy meals fast using just five ingredients.

If you don't have a lot of time to cook, this book is for you.

Creating delicious and easy meals with only 5 ingredients is the new trend.

These 5 ingredients (or less) recipes are very fast and easy but taste like you put loads of time and effort into them. Each one needs just a handful of ingredients, plus salt, pepper, and cooking oil in some cases, so they won't be a strain on your family budget.

This book is all about the ingenious combination of a few ingredients. Their combination can produce amazing results and give you an explosion of flavor with a minimum of effort.

Many sweet and savory recipes with few ingredients are just waiting to be tried. Super easy, you'll make them quickly and everyone will be amazed.

Fancy a sweet treat but few ingredients at home?

Desserts with 3 ingredients, but also main courses that you will cook in no time while making it easy on your budget. Sometimes you just need to make the most of a few raw materials to prepare outstanding meals.

Recipes with only 5 ingredients are waiting for you, enjoy!

5-Ingredient Recipes

Cauliflower Toast with Avocado

Time required:
40 minutes

Servings: 03

INGREDIENTS

3 large eggs

*3 big head
cauliflower, grated*

*3 medium avocados,
pitted and chopped*

*1 cup mozzarella
cheese, shredded*

*Salt and black
pepper, to taste*

STEPS FOR COOKING

1. Preheat the oven to 420°F, then line a baking sheet with parchment.

2. Place the cauliflower in a microwave-safe bowl and microwave for about 7 minutes on high.

3. Spread on paper towels to drain after the cauliflower has completely cooled and press with a clean towel to remove excess moisture.

4. Put the cauliflower back in the bowl and stir in the mozzarella cheese and egg.

5. Season with salt and black pepper and stir until well combined.

6. Spoon the mixture onto the baking sheet in two rounded squares, as evenly as possible.

7. Bake for about 20 minutes until golden brown on the edges. 8. Mash

the avocado with a pinch of salt and black pepper.

8. Spread the avocado onto the cauliflower toast and serve.

Almond Butter Brownies

Time required:
30 minutes

———————

Servings: 04

INGREDIENTS

1 scoop protein powder

2 tbsp. cocoa powder

1/2 cup almond butter, melted

1 cup bananas, overripe

STEPS FOR COOKING

1. Preheat the oven to 350 F/ 176 C, then spray the brownie tray with cooking spray.
2. Add all the ingredients into the blender, mix until smooth.
3. Pour batter into the prepared dish and bake in preheated oven for 20 minutes.
4. Serve and enjoy.

Pumpkin Pancakes

Time required:
20 minutes

Servings: 08

INGREDIENTS

2 squares puff pastry

6 tbsp pumpkin filling

2 small eggs, beaten

¼ tsp cinnamon

STEPS FOR COOKING

1. Preheat the Airfryer to 360 F and roll out a square of puff pastry.

2. Layer it with pumpkin pie filling, leaving about 1/4 -inch space around the edges.

3. Cut it up into equal-sized square pieces and cover the gaps with beaten egg.

4. Arrange the squares into a baking dish and cook for about 12 minutes.

5. Sprinkle some cinnamon and serve.

Kale Smoothie

Time required:
5 minutes

Servings: 02

INGREDIENTS

2 cups chopped kale leaves

1 banana, peeled

1 cup frozen strawberries

1 cup unsweetened almond milk

4 Medjool dates, pitted and chopped

STEPS FOR COOKING

1. Put all the ingredients in a food processor, then blitz until glossy and smooth.

2. Serve immediately.

Tiramisu Chia Pudding

Time required:
20 minutes

Servings: 01

INGREDIENTS

¼ cup Chia Seeds

2 tsp Instant Coffee

2 tbsp Coconut
Cream

¾ cup Water

1 tbsp Erythritol

1 tsp Powdered
Cinnamon

STEPS FOR COOKING

1. Combine all ingredients in a mason jar, then shake until well blended.

2. Chill for at least 20 minutes.

Apple - Lemon Bowl

Time required:
20 minutes

Servings: 02

INGREDIENTS

6 apples
3 tablespoons
walnuts
7 dates Lemon juice
1/2 teaspoon
cinnamon

STEPS FOR COOKING

1. Root the apples, then break them into wide bits.
2. In a food cup, put seeds, part of the lime juice, almonds, spices, and three-quarters of the apples. Thinly slice until finely ground.
3. Apply the remaining apples and lemon juice and make slices.

Bacon Mini Frittata

Time required:
40 minutes

Servings: 12

INGREDIENTS

1 cup chopped asparagus (about 7-8)

4 slices of bacon cut into cubes

2 tablespoons of chopped onions

8 eggs, beaten

1/2 cup (120 ml) coconut milk

Salt and pepper to taste

STEPS FOR COOKING

1. Preheat the oven to 350 degrees Fahrenheit (175 degrees Celsius).
2. Cook chopped bacon in a frying pan.
3. Mix all the chopped vegetables, cooked bacon, scrambled eggs, and coconut milk together in a large bowl.
4. Pour the mixture into muffin cups (makes 12 small quiches).
5. Bake for 25-30 minutes.

Chocolate Peanut Butter Shake

Time required:
5 minutes

Servings: 02

INGREDIENTS

2 bananas

3 Tablespoons peanut butter

1 cup almond milk

3 Tablespoons cacao powder

STEPS FOR COOKING

1. Combine all the ingredients in a blender until smooth, then serve.

Ham Muffins

Time required:
25 minutes

Servings: 04

INGREDIENTS

3 oz ham, chopped

4 eggs, beaten

2 tablespoon
coconut flour

½ teaspoon dried
oregano

¼ teaspoon dried
cilantro

Cooking spray

STEPS FOR COOKING

1. Spray the muffin's molds with cooking spray.

2. In a bowl, mix the beaten eggs, coconut flour, dried oregano, cilantro, and ham.

3. When the liquid is homogenous, pour in it the prepared muffin molds.

4. Bake the muffins for 15 minutes at 360F

5. Chill the cooked meal well and only after this remove it from the molds.

Nori Salmon Handroll

Time required:
10 minutes

Servings: 01

INGREDIENTS

2 ounces wild canned salmon

1 toasted nori sheet

1/4 avocado

1 cucumber

1 green onion

STEPS FOR COOKING

1. Slice avocado and cucumber and finely chop the green onion.
2. Put the nori paper on a cutting board, and layer the avocado, fish, 2 slices of cucumber, and green onion.
3. Wrap the paper around.

Breakfast Cheesy Sausage

Time required:
25 minutes

Servings: 01

INGREDIENTS

1 pork sausage link, cut open and casing discarded

½ teaspoon thyme

½ teaspoon sage

½ cup mozzarella cheese, shredded

Sea salt and black pepper, to taste

STEPS FOR COOKING

1. Mix the sausage meat with thyme, sage, mozzarella cheese, sea salt, and black pepper.

2. Shape the mixture into 2 equal-sized patties and transfer to a hot pan.

3. Cook for about 5 minutes per side and dish out to serve.

Crusty Grilled Corn

Time required:
25 minutes

Servings: 04

INGREDIENTS

2 corn cobs

1/3 cup Vegenaise

1 small handful of Cilantro

½ cup breadcrumbs

1 teaspoon lemon juice

STEPS FOR COOKING

1. Preheat the gas grill on high heat.
2. Add corn grill to the grill and continue grilling until it turns golden-brown on all sides.

Creamy Potato Spread

Time required:
25 minutes

———

Servings: 06

INGREDIENTS

*1 lb sweet potatoes,
peeled and chopped*

*¾ tbsp fresh chives,
chopped*

½ tsp paprika

1 tbsp garlic, minced

1 cup tomato puree

Pepper and Salt

STEPS FOR COOKING

1. Add all ingredients except chives into the inner pot and stir well.
2. Seal pot with the lid and cook on high for 15 minutes.
3. Once done, allow to release pressure naturally for 10 minutes, then release remaining using quick release. Remove lid.
4. Transfer instant pot sweet potato mixture into the food processor and process until smooth.
5. Garnish with chives and serve.

Garlic and Kale Platter

Time required:
15 minutes

Servings: 04

INGREDIENTS

1 bunch kale

2 tablespoons olive oil

4 garlic cloves, minced

STEPS FOR COOKING

1. Carefully tear the kale into bite-sized portions, making sure to remove the stem.

2. Discard the stems.

3. Take a large-sized pot and place it over medium heat.

4. Add olive oil and let the oil heat up, then add garlic and stir for 2 minutes.

5. Add kale and cook for 5-10 minutes.

6. Serve!

Almond Bread

Time required:
40 minutes

Servings: 20

INGREDIENTS

6 eggs, separated

1/4 teaspoon cream of tartar

3 teaspoons baking powder

4 tablespoons butter, melted

1 1/2 cups almond flour

1/4 teaspoon salt

STEPS FOR COOKING

1. Preheat the oven to 375 F. Grease 8*4-inch loaf pan with butter and set aside. Add egg whites and cream of tartar in a large bowl and beat until soft peaks form.

2. Add almond flour, baking powder, egg yolks, butter, and salt in a food processor and process until combined.

3. Add 1/3 of egg white mixture into the almond flour mixture and process until combined. Now add the remaining egg white mixture and process gently to combine.

4. Pour batter into the prepared loaf pan, then bake for 30 minutes. Slice and serve.

Mozzarella Chips

Time required:
10 minutes

Servings: 08

INGREDIENTS

*4 phyllo dough
sheets*

*4 oz mozzarella,
shredded*

*1 tablespoon olive
oil*

STEPS FOR COOKING

1. Place 2 phyllo sheets in the pan and brush it with a sprinkle of mozzarella.

2. Then cover the cheese with 2 remaining phyllo sheets.

3. Brush the top of Phyllo with olive oil and cut on 8 squares.

4. Bake the chips for l0 minutes at 363F or until they are light brown.

Broccoli Stir Fry

Time required:
25 minutes

Servings: 02

INGREDIENTS

1 tablespoon coconut oil

2 cups broccoli florets

1 tablespoon low-sodium soy sauce

¼ teaspoon garlic powder

Ground black pepper, as required

STEPS FOR COOKING

1. In a large pan, melt the coconut oil over medium heat and stir in the broccoli.

2. Cover the pan, then cook for 10 minutes, stirring occasionally.

3. Stir in the soy sauce and spices and cook for about 5 minutes.

4. Serve hot.

Wrapped Plums

Time required:
5 minutes

Servings: 08

INGREDIENTS

2 ounces prosciutto, cut into 16 pieces

4 plums, quartered

1 tablespoon chives, chopped

A pinch of red pepper flakes, crushed

STEPS FOR COOKING

1. Wrap each plum quarter in a prosciutto slice, arrange them all on a platter, sprinkle the chives and pepper flakes all over.

2. Serve.

Fried Apple

Time required:
20 minutes

Servings: 04

INGREDIENTS

1 cup of coconut oil

¼ cup date paste

2 tablespoons ground cinnamon

4 apples, peeled and sliced, cored

STEPS FOR COOKING

1. Place a large-sized skillet over medium heat.

2. Add oil and allow it to heat. Add date paste and cinnamon and stir.

3. Add the apples and fry until crispy, for 5-8 minutes.

4. Serve and enjoy!

Paprika Sweet Potato

Time required:
21 minutes

Servings: 02

INGREDIENTS

2 sweet potatoes

2 teaspoons sweet paprika

1/2 teaspoon oregano, dried

1 teaspoon chili powder

1 teaspoon chives, chopped

1/2 cup of water

STEPS FOR COOKING

1. Pour water into the instant pot and insert a steamer rack.
2. Put potatoes on the rack and close the lid.
3. Set Manual mode (High pressure) and cook for 11 minutes. Then use quick pressure release.
4. Transfer the potatoes to the plate, cut into halves, sprinkle the rest of the ingredients on top, and serve.

Tomato Basil Spaghetti

Time required:
25 minutes

_____

Servings: 04

INGREDIENTS

15-ounce cooked great northern beans

10.5-ounces cherry tomatoes halved

1 small white onion, peeled, diced

1 tablespoon minced garlic

8 basil leaves, chopped

2 tablespoons olive oil

1-pound spaghetti

STEPS FOR COOKING

1. Take a large pot half full with salty water, place it over medium-high heat, bring it to a boil, add spaghetti and cook for 10 to 12 minutes until tender.

2. Then drain spaghetti into a colander and reserve 1 cup of pasta liquid.

3. Take a large skillet pan, place it over medium-high heat, add oil, and when hot, add onion, tomatoes, basil, and garlic and cook for 5 minutes until vegetables have turned tender.

4. Add cooked spaghetti and beans, pour in pasta water, stir until just mixed and cook for 2 minutes until hot.

5. Serve straight away.

Worcestershire Pork Chops

Time required:
15 minutes

Servings: 03

INGREDIENTS

2 tablespoons
Worcestershire
sauce

8 oz pork loin chops

1 tablespoon lemon
juice

1 teaspoon olive oil

STEPS FOR COOKING

1. Mix up together Worcestershire sauce, lemon juice, and olive oil.
2. Brush the pork loin chops with the sauce mixture from each side.
3. Preheat the grill to 395F.
4. Place the pork chops in the grill and cook them for 5 minutes.
5. Then flip the pork chops on another side and brush with the remaining sauce mixture.
6. Grill the meat for 7-8 minutes more.

Baked Chicken Wings

Time required:
60 minutes

Servings: 04

INGREDIENTS

2 lbs chicken wings

1 tbsp. lemon-pepper seasoning

2 tbsp butter, melted

4 tbsp olive oil

STEPS FOR COOKING

1. Preheat the oven to 400 F.
2. Toss chicken wings with olive oil.
3. Arrange chicken wings on a baking tray and bake for 50 minutes.
4. In a small bowl, mix together lemon pepper seasoning and butter.
5. Remove wings from oven and brush with butter and seasoning mixture.
6. Serve and enjoy.

Broccoli Bacon Salad with Onions and Coconut Cream

Time required:
40 minutes

Servings: 06

INGREDIENTS

1 pound of broccoli

4 small red onions or 2 large slices

20 bacon, cut into small pieces

1 cup coconut cream

Salt, to taste

STEPS FOR COOKING

1. Cook the bacon first, then cook the onions in the bacon fat.
2. Cook the broccoli florets.
3. Add bacon chunks, onions, and cauliflower florets, along with coconut cream and salt to taste.
4. Serve at room temperature.

Thyme and Lemon Couscous

Time required:
15 minutes

Servings: 06

INGREDIENTS

.25 cup Chopped parsley

1.5 cup Couscous

2 tbsp. Chopped thyme

Juice and zest of a lemon

2.75 cup Vegetable stock

STEPS FOR COOKING

1. Take out a pot and add in the thyme, lemon juice, and vegetable stock. Stir in the couscous after it has gotten to a boil and then take off the heat.

2. Allow sitting covered until it can take in all of the liquid. Then fluff up with a form.

3. Stir in the parsley and lemon zest, then serve warm.

Sage Salmon Fillet

Time required:
25 minutes

Servings: 01

INGREDIENTS

4 oz salmon fillet

½ teaspoon salt

1 teaspoon sesame oil

½ teaspoon same

STEPS FOR COOKING

1. Rub the fillet with salt and sage.
2. Place the fish in the tray and sprinkle it with sesame oil.
3. Cook the fish for 25 minutes at 365F.
4. Flip the fish carefully onto another side after 12 minutes of cooking.

Eggs Baked in an Avocado

Time required:
17minutes

Servings: 02

INGREDIENTS

1 avocado

2 egg yolks

2 teaspoons olive oil or coconut oil

Salt, pepper, spices / other herbs to taste

STEPS FOR COOKING

1. Preheat the oven to 400 ° F.
2. Cut the avocado in half. You don't need the core.
3. Break the eggs into a bowl.
4. Scoop out each egg yolk and place half an avocado.
5. Pour 1 teaspoon of olive oil over each avocado egg yolk.
6. Bake for 12 minutes.
7. Sprinkle with salt and pepper and whatever herbs and spices you want to add.

Shrimp Ginger Cucumber with Fried Rice

Time required:
15 minutes

Servings: 01

INGREDIENTS

1 large cucumber, peeled and sliced into round slices

10-15 shrimp / large shrimp

1 teaspoon grated fresh ginger

Salt and pepper to taste

Coconut oil for cooking

STEPS FOR COOKING

1. Put a tablespoon of coconut oil in a frying pan over medium heat.
2. Add ginger and cucumber and sauté for 2-3 minutes.
3. Add shrimp and cook until pink.
4. Add salt to taste and serve.

5 Ingredients Pasta

Time required:
40 minutes

Servings: 05

INGREDIENTS

1 (25 oz.) jar
marinara sauce

Olive oil, as needed

1 pound dry vegan
pasta

1 pound assorted
vegetables, like red
onion, zucchini, and
tomatoes

¼ cup prepared
hummus

Salt, to taste

STEPS FOR COOKING

1. Preheat the oven to 400 degrees F,
   then grease a large baking sheet.

2. Arrange the vegetables in a single
   layer on the baking sheet and sprinkle
   with olive oil and salt.

3. Transfer into the oven and roast the
   vegetables for about 15 minutes.

4. Boil salted water in a large pot and
   cook the pasta according to the
   package directions.

5. Drain the water when the pasta is
   tender and put the pasta in a
   colander.

6. Mix together the marinara sauce and
   hummus in a large pot to make a
   creamy sauce.

7. Stir in the cooked vegetables and pasta to the sauce and toss to coat well.

8. Dish out in a bowl and serve warm.

French Onion Soup

Time required:
40 minutes

Servings: 06

INGREDIENTS

5 tablespoons butter

500g brown onion medium

4 drops liquid stevia

4 tablespoons olive oil

3 cups beef stock

STEPS FOR COOKING

1. Put the butter and olive oil in a large pot over medium-low heat and add onions and salt.

2. Cook for about 5 minutes and stir in stevia.

3. Cook for another 5 minutes and add beef stock.

4. Reduce the heat to low, then simmer for about 25 minutes.

5. Dish out into soup bowls and serve hot.

Cream of Mushroom Soup

Time required:
36 minutes

Servings: 02

INGREDIENTS

*2 cups cauliflower
florets*

*1 2/3 cup plain
almond milk*

1 tsp onion powder

1/2 tsp EVOO

*1 1/2 cups button
mushrooms, diced*

*1/2 yellow onion,
chopped*

STEPS FOR COOKING

1. Boil the cauliflower in a pot with almond milk and onion powder. Season with salt and pepper, then drop to a simmer and cook until the cauliflower is just tender 5-7 minutes. Blend this mixture until very smooth in a blender.

2. Sauté the mushrooms and onions in a separate pan in the oil. Cook on high heat, so that the vegetables can gain color and the mushrooms will leach out some of their liquid.

3. Add the cauliflower puree to the mushrooms after 7-8 minutes, then bring to a boil. Lower the heat and cover, then cook until the soup is thick and creamy, 10-12 minutes.

4. Season and serve.

Grilled Eggplant Steaks

Time required:
25 minutes

Servings: 02

INGREDIENTS

4 Roma tomatoes, diced

8 ounces cashew cream

2 eggplants

1 tablespoon olive oil

1 cup parsley, chopped

1 cucumber, diced

Salt and pepper to taste

STEPS FOR COOKING

1. Slice eggplants into three thick steaks, drizzle with oil, and season with salt and pepper.
2. Grill in a pan for 4 minutes per side.
3. Top with remaining ingredients.
4. Serve and enjoy!

Coconut Chicken

Time required:
5 minutes

Servings: 04

INGREDIENTS

6 oz chicken fillet

¼ cup of sparkling water

1 egg

3 tablespoons coconut flakes

1 tablespoon coconut oil

1 teaspoon Greek Seasoning

STEPS FOR COOKING

1. Cut the chicken fillet into small pieces (nuggets).
2. Then crack the egg in the bowl and whisk it.
3. Mix up together egg and sparkling water.
4. Add Greek seasoning and stir gently.
5. Dip the chicken nuggets in the egg mixture and then coat in the coconut flakes.
6. Melt the coconut oil in the skillet and heat it up until it is shimmering.
7. Then add prepared chicken nuggets.
8. Roast them for 1 minute from each or until they are light brown.

INGREDIENTS	STEPS FOR COOKING

9. Dry the cooked chicken nuggets with the help of the paper towel and transfer them to the serving plates.

Shrimp and Broccoli

Time required:
17 minutes

Servings: 02

INGREDIENTS

1/2 lb shrimp

1 tsp fresh lemon juice

2 tbsp butter

2 garlic cloves, minced

1 cup broccoli florets

Salt

STEPS FOR COOKING

1. Melt butter in a pan over medium heat, then add garlic and broccoli to the pan and cook for 3-4 minutes.
2. Add shrimp and cook for 3-4 minutes.
3. Add lemon juice and salt, then stir well.
4. Serve and enjoy.

Tofu Nuggets with Barbecue Glaze

Time required:
35 minutes

Servings: 09

INGREDIENTS

32 ounces tofu

1 cup quick vegan barbecue sauce

STEPS FOR COOKING

1. Set the oven to 425F.
2. Next, slice the tofu and blot the tofu with clean towels, then slice and dice the tofu and completely eliminate the water from the tofu material.
3. Stir the tofu with the vegan barbecue sauce, and place the tofu on a baking sheet.
4. Bake the tofu for fifteen minutes. Afterward, stir the tofu and bake the tofu for an additional ten minutes.
5. Enjoy!

Yummy Turkey Meatballs

Time required:
25 minutes

Servings: 04

INGREDIENTS

¼ yellow onion,
finely diced

1 14-oz can of
artichoke hearts,
diced

1 lb. ground turkey

1 tsp dried parsley

1 tsp oil

4 tbsp fresh basil,
finely chopped

Pepper, and salt to
taste

STEPS FOR COOKING

1. Grease a cookie sheet, then preheat
   the oven to 350F.

2. On medium fire, place a nonstick
   medium saucepan and sauté artichoke
   hearts and diced onions for 5 minutes
   or until onions are soft.

3. Remove from fire and let cool.

4. Meanwhile, in a big bowl, mix with
   hands parsley, basil, and ground
   turkey. Season to taste.

5. Once the onion mixture has cooled,
   add it into the bowl and mix
   thoroughly.

6. With an ice cream scooper, scoop
   ground turkey and form it into balls,
   make around 6 balls.

7. Place on prepped cookie sheet, pop in the oven and bake until cooked through around 15-20 minutes.

8. Remove from pan, serve and enjoy.

Healthy Poached Trout

Time required:
10 minutes

Servings: 02

INGREDIENTS

1 8-OZ boneless,
skin-on trout fillet

2 cups chicken broth
or water

2 leeks, halved

6-8 slices lemon

Salt and pepper to
taste

STEPS FOR COOKING

1. On medium fire, place a large nonstick skillet and arrange leeks and lemons on a pan in a layer. Cover with soup stock or water and bring to a simmer.

2. Meanwhile, season trout with pepper and salt, then place trout on a simmering pan of water. Cover and cook until trout is flaky, around 8 minutes.

3. In a seeing platter, spoon leek and lemons on the bottom of the plate, top with trout, and spoon sauce into the plate. Serve and enjoy.

Avocado Cucumber Soup

Time required:
20 minutes

Servings: 03

INGREDIENTS

1 large cucumber, peeled and sliced

¾ cup water

¼ cup lemon juice

2 garlic cloves

6 green onion

2 avocados, pitted

Salt and pepper

STEPS FOR COOKING

1. Add all ingredients into the blender and blend until smooth and creamy.
2. Place in refrigerator for 30 minutes.
3. Stir well and serve chilled.

Oregano and Pesto Lamb

Time required:
25 minutes

Servings: 04

INGREDIENTS

2 pounds pork
shoulder, boneless
and cubed

¼ cup olive oil

2 teaspoons
oregano, dried

¼ cup lemon juice

3 garlic cloves,
minced

2 teaspoons basil
pesto

Salt and black
pepper to the taste

STEPS FOR COOKING

1. Heat up a pan with the oil over
   medium-high heat, then add the pork,
   and brown for 5 minutes.

2. Add the rest of the ingredients, cook
   for 20 minutes more, tossing the mix
   from time to time, divide between
   plates and serve.

Buttery Shrimp

Time required:
20 minutes

Servings: 04

INGREDIENTS

1 1/2 lbs shrimp

1 tbsp Italian
seasoning

1 lemon, sliced

1 stick butter,
melted

STEPS FOR COOKING

1. Add all ingredients into the large
    mixing bowl and toss well. 2. Transfer
    the shrimp mixture to a baking tray.

2. Bake at 350 F for 15 minutes.

3. Serve and enjoy.

Salted Caramel Chocolate Cups

Time required:
7 minutes

Servings: 12

INGREDIENTS

¼ teaspoon sea salt
granules

1 cup dark chocolate
chips, unsweetened

2 teaspoons coconut
oil

6 tablespoons
caramel sauce

STEPS FOR COOKING

1. Take a heatproof bowl, add chocolate chips and oil, stir until mixed, then microwave for 1 minute until melted, stir chocolate and continue heating in the microwave for 30 seconds.

2. Take twelve mini muffin tins, line them with muffin liners, spoon a little bit of chocolate mixture into the tins, spread the chocolate in the bottom and along the sides, and freeze for 10 minutes until set.

3. Then fill each cup with ½ tablespoon of caramel sauce, cover with remaining chocolate and freeze for another 2salt0 minutes until set.

4. When ready to eat, peel off liner from the cup, sprinkle with sauce, and serve.

Warm Peach Compote

Time required:
5 minutes

Servings: 04

INGREDIENTS

4 peaches, peeled
and chopped

1 tbsp water

½ tbsp cornstarch

1 tsp vanilla

STEPS FOR COOKING

1. Add water, vanilla, and peaches into the instant pot.
2. Seal pot with lid and cook on high for 1 minute.
3. Once done, allow to release pressure naturally. Remove lid.
4. In a small bowl, whisk together 1 tbsp of water and cornstarch and pour into the pot and stir well.
5. Serve and enjoy.

Vanilla Custard

Time required:
20 minutes

Servings: 02

INGREDIENTS

8 egg yolks

1 cup unsweetened almond milk

1 teaspoon vanilla extract

10 stevia extract drops (optional)

6 tablespoons melted coconut oil or unsalted butter

STEPS FOR COOKING

1. In a large, heatproof bowl, whisk the eggs, and then add the milk, vanilla, and honey.
2. Slowly mix in the melted coconut oil.
3. Now place this bowl over a pan of simmering water.
4. Insert a cooking thermometer into the pudding. Once the thermometer reads 140°F, remove the custard from the water bath.
5. Serve it warm or chilled.

Peanut Brittle

Time required:
25 minutes

___

Servings: 04

INGREDIENTS

1 cup peanuts,
salted and roasted

2 oz butter

3 oz swerve
sweetener

1 tsp vanilla extract

STEPS FOR COOKING

1. Line a cookie sheet with wax paper and spread out the peanuts.

2. Using a small saucepan over medium heat, combine the butter, sweetener, and vanilla.

3. Cook until it reaches the caramelized stage and is deep brown in color. Do not undercook to avoid making your brittle grainy.

4. Pour the caramel over the spread peanuts and let it cool for 30 minutes to an hour. Once it hardens, break into pieces before serving.

Watermelon Mint Popsicles

Time required:
25 minutes

Servings: 08

INGREDIENTS

20 mint leaves, diced

6 cups watermelon chunks

3 tablespoons lime juice

STEPS FOR COOKING

1. Add watermelon in a food processor along with lime juice and then pulse for 15 seconds until smooth.

2. Pass the watermelon mixture through a strainer placed over a bowl, remove the seeds and then stir mint into the collected watermelon mixture.

3. Take eight Popsicle molds, pour in prepared watermelon mixture, and freeze for 2 hours until slightly firm.

4. Then insert popsicle sticks and continue freezing for 6 hours until solid.

5. Serve straight away.

Creamy Strawberries

Time required:
5 minutes

Servings: 04

INGREDIENTS

6 tablespoons almond butter

1 tablespoon Erythritol

1 cup milk

1 teaspoon vanilla extract

1 cup strawberries, sliced

STEPS FOR COOKING

1. Pour milk into the saucepan.
2. Add Erythritol, vanilla extract, and almond butter.
3. With the help of the hand mixer, mix up the liquid until smooth and bring it to a boil.
4. Now, remove the mixture from the heat and let it cool.
5. The cooled mixture will be thick.
6. Put the strawberries in the serving glasses and top with the thick almond butter dip.

Coconut Bars

Time required:
45 minutes

Servings: 02

INGREDIENTS

*1 large scoop
protein powder,
vanilla flavored*

*4 oz. dark chocolate
chips, unsweetened*

*1 cup coconut,
flaked*

*¾ cup coconut oil,
melted*

*1½ cups macadamia
nuts, raw*

STEPS FOR COOKING

1. Using an 8-inch pan, cover with baking paper or a non-stick mat.

2. In a food blender set to high, blend the macadamia nuts and coconut oil until evenly mixed.

3. Combine the protein powder, chocolate chips, and coconut until mixed thoroughly.

4. Transfer the batter to the prepped pan and freeze for half an hour.

5. After it's set, slice into 14 individual bars. 6. Thaw for 10 minutes before serving.

Boston Baked Beans Candy

Time required:
60 minutes

Servings: 06

INGREDIENTS

2 cup peanuts, raw

1 cup allulose

½ cup water

STEPS FOR COOKING

1. Place the entire ingredients in a large skillet. Cook over moderate heat until the water is evaporated, stirring every now and then.

2. Pour the mixture on a large-sized cookie sheet and bake in the oven for 20 minutes at 325°F. Break apart, if required.

Chocolate Rice

Time required:
20 minutes

Servings: 04

INGREDIENTS

1 cup of rice

1 tbsp cocoa powder

2 tbsp maple syrup

2 cups almond milk

STEPS FOR COOKING

1. Add all ingredients into the inner pot of the instant pot and stir well.

2. Seal pot with lid and cook on high for 20 minutes.

3. Once done, allow to release pressure naturally for 10 minutes, then release remaining using quick release. Remove lid.

4. Stir and serve.

Greek Yogurt Muesli Parfaits

Time required:
10 minutes

Servings: 04

INGREDIENTS

4 cups Greek yogurt

1 cup whole wheat muesli

2 cups fresh berries of your choice

STEPS FOR COOKING

1. Layer the four classes with Greek yogurt at the bottom, muesli on top, and berries.

2. Repeat the layers until the glass is filled, then place in the fridge for at least hours to chill.